Jazz Styles
Level Three
Supplement to All Piano and Keyboard Methods

Compiled and Edited by Wesley Schaum
Arrangements by Wesley Schaum and Jeff Schaum

Foreword

Jazz styles, evolving over many years, encompass a broad range including ragtime, blues, boogie, swing and rock. A casual, improvisational attitude is the common thread. The syncopated rhythms and harmonies have remained popular for many generations and provide fascinating educational material.

This collection includes arrangements of authentic ragtime by Scott Joplin, Charles Hunter and Joseph F. Lamb as well as original works by Duane Hampton and Wesley Schaum.

Index

SCHAUM PUBLICATIONS, INC.
10235 N. Port Washington Rd. • Mequon, WI 53092

www.schaumpiano.net

© Copyright 1966, 1982, 1996 and 2000 by Schaum Publications, Inc., Mequon, Wisconsin
International Copyright Secured • All Rights Reserved • Printed in U.S.A.

WARNING : The reproduction of any part of this publication without prior written consent of Schaum Publications, Inc. is prohibited by U.S. Copyright Law and subject to penalty. This prohibition includes all forms of printed media (including any method of photocopy), all forms of electronic media (including computer images), all forms of film media (including filmstrips, transparencies, slides and movies), all forms of sound recordings (including cassette tapes and compact disks), and all forms of video media (including video tapes and video disks).

Easy Winners

Scott Joplin
Arr. by Wesley Schaum and Jeff Schaum

Andantino ♩ = 108-116

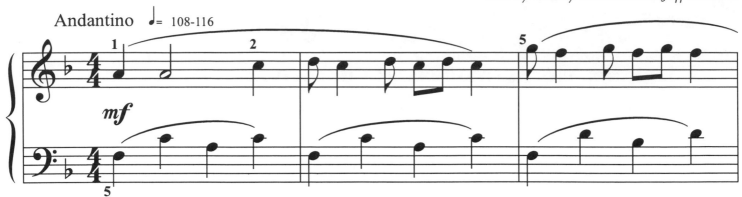

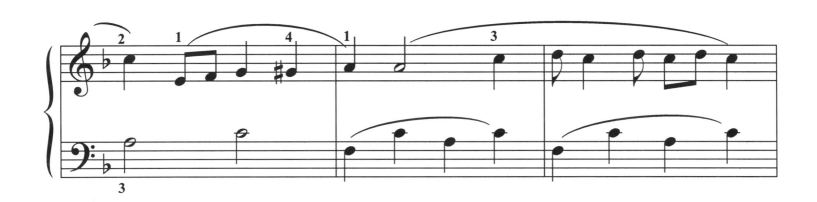

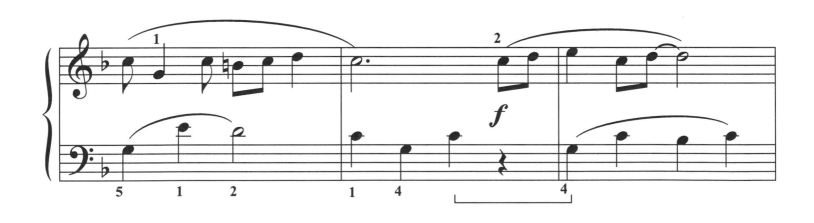

Boogie Fast

Vivace 𝅗𝅥 = 100-112

Duane Hampton

Boogie Strut

Duane Hampton

Allegretto ♩= 120-138 (swing 8ths)

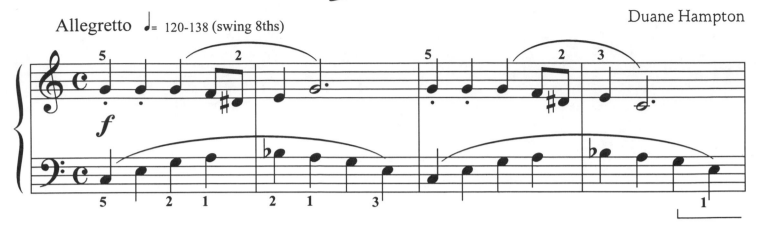

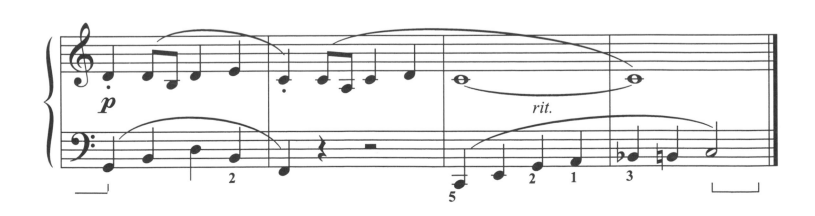

Ramblin'

Grazioso ♩= 120-138 (swing 8ths)

Wesley Schaum

Honeysuckle Rag

Joseph F. Lamb
Arr. by Wesley Schaum and Jeff Schaum

9

Giant Burger Blues

Wesley Schaum

Doloroso ♩= 96-108 (swing 8ths)

Hush Puppy Blues

Wesley Schaum

Allegro moderato ♩= 108-120 (swing 8ths)

Come Alive

Wesley Schaum

Peacherine Rag

Scott Joplin
Arr. by Wesley Schaum and Jeff Schaum

Moderato ♩ = 116-126

Jalopy Cat

Animato ♩= 76-88

Wesley Schaum

Rollin' Rhythm

Wesley Schaum

Runaround

Wesley Schaum

Tennessee Tantalizer

Charles Hunter
Arr. by Wesley Schaum and Jeff Schaum

21

27 Flavor Blues

Moderato ♩= 84-100 (swing 8ths)

Wesley Schaum

Successful Schaum Sheet Music

This is a Partial List — Showing Level 3 and selected Level 4

• = Original Form   * = Big Notes   ✓ = Chord Symbols

LEVEL

AMERICAN – PATRIOTIC SOLOS

58-30	✓ANCHORS AWEIGH	Zimmerman	3
61-35	✓BATTLE HYMN of the REPUBLIC	Steffe	4
58-44	✓CAISSONS SONG (U.S. Field Artillery)		3
58-21	✓DIXIE	Emmett	3
58-11	NATIONAL EMBLEM MARCH		3
58-45	✓SEMPER FIDELIS (U.S. Marines)	Sousa	3
61-36	✓STARS and STRIPES FOREVER	Sousa	4
58-18	✓STAR-SPANGLED BANNER	Commemorative Ed.	3
61-13	YANKEE DOODLE	Theme & Variations	4
58-10	✓YOU'RE A GRAND OLD FLAG	Cohan	3

ANIMALS and BIRDS

58-62	• BARNYARD BUDDIES	Costley	3
58-56	• BUCKING BRONCO (L.H. Melody)	King	3
61-51	• CACTUS CAT	Schwabe	4
61-38	• FROG IN THE FOG (L.H. Melody)	Endres	4

BOOGIE

58-25	• BAGPIPE BOOGIE (Grace Notes)	Leach	3
58-05	• BEACH BALL BOOGIE	Schaum	4

CHRISTMAS

70-06	✓SANTA'S ON HIS WAY	Schaum	4

CIRCUS

58-42	• GREASE PAINT GERTIE	McKinley	3

CLASSICS

61-41	AVE VERUM	Mozart	4
61-42	FIRST SYMPHONY THEME (4th Mvt)	Brahms	4
58-24	* JOY PRELUDE ("Jesu Joy of Man's Desiring")	Bach	3
61-09	MINUET MEDLEY (G Major - G Minor)	Bach	4
61-14	BEETHOVEN'S 5th SYMPHONY (1st Mvt. Theme)		4
58-39	BEETHOVEN'S 7th SYMPHONY (2nd Mvt. Theme)		3
61-02	FUR ELISE	Beethoven	4
61-11	SONATA IN C (Both Hands in Treble)	Mozart	4
58-15	SYMPHONY No. 40 (First Theme)	Mozart	3
61-46	TALES FROM THE VIENNA WOODS	Strauss	4
61-45	TRUMPET CONCERTO THEME	Haydn	4
61-08	TURKISH MARCH ("Rondo alla Turka")	Mozart	4
61-30	DANCE OF THE HOURS	Ponchielli	4
58-34	MINUET IN D	Salieri	3
61-34	WATER MUSIC (Bouree)	Handel	3

COUNTRY/WESTERN

58-38	AMERICAN INDIAN SUITE	4 Tribal Themes	3
58-33	*✓YELLOW ROSE, The	Traditional	3

DESCRIPTIVE MUSIC

61-49	• ALMOST BAROQUE	Revezoulis	4
61-48	• APPALACHIAN SUNRISE	Schwabe	4
61-37	• BAREFOOT FROLIC	Cahn	4
58-48	• COUNTY FAIR	Leach	3
61-56	• LOST ISLAND	King	4
61-43	• MORNING'S PROMISE	Cahn	4
58-53	• PERPETUAL MOTION (6/8 Time)	Cahn	3
58-60	• PIANO PIZAZZ	Cahn	3
58-47	• SLEEPY ALARM CLOCK	Cahn	3

DUETS   (1 Piano, 4 Hands)

71-03	BIRTHDAY BOUQUET	Theme & Variations	4
71-01	ENTERTAINER	Joplin	4
71-08	• OOM-PAH-PAH (Solo and Duet)	Cahn	3

ETHNIC MUSIC

58-07	✓HAVA NAGILA (Minor Key)	Israeli Folk Dance	3
61-24	TARANTELLA (6/8 Time)	Italian Folk Dance	4

LEVEL

HALLOWEEN

61-05	FUNERAL MARCH of a MARIONETTE	Gounod	4
58-41	• GHOSTLY JIVE (Minor Key)	Leach	3
58-59	• WACKY WITCHES	King	3

JAZZ

58-19	• COUNTRY ROCK	Jones	3
61-18	• HAPPY TRUMPET	Muniz	4
80-08	✓IN THE MOOD	Garland	3
61-52	• JAZZ SPREE	Polhamus	4
61-34	• MIZ TUTTLE SHUFFLE	Leach	4
58-57	• RUNAROUND ROCK	Biel	3

MARCHES

61-04	• CARAVAN (6/8 Time)	Kahl	4
61-53	• FESTIVE FANFARE	Cahn	4
58-50	✓WASHINGTON POST MARCH	Sousa	3

MINOR KEY

58-43	* •DRIZZLY DAY (Minor Key)	Holmes	3
61-26	✓SCARBOROUGH FAIR	English Folk Song	4
58-49	• SUMMER SCHERZO	Leach	3

MOVIE THEMES

80-02	OVER THE RAINBOW (from "Wizard of Oz")	Arlen	3

OLDIES but GOODIES

58-02	✓GIVE MY REGARDS TO BROADWAY	Cohan	3

RAGTIME

61-33	• BABY BRONTOSAURUS RAG	McKinley	4
61-10	✓ENTERTAINER	Joplin	4
58-51	• RAMBLIN' RAG	King	3

ROMANTIC MOOD

58-31	ASPIRATION	Schumann	3
61-55	CHERISH THE MOMENT	Nelson	4
58-01	✓FASCINATION WALTZ	Marchetti	3
61-40	INTERMEZZO IN D	Sor	4
58-36	✓LET ME CALL YOU SWEETHEART	Friedman	3
61-03	MELODY IN F (2/4 Time)	Rubinstein	4

SACRED

61-17	DONA NOBIS PACEM ("Grant Us Thy Peace")		4
58-32	✓JUST A CLOSER WALK WITH THEE	Spiritual	3

SHOW TUNES

80-21	✓SEND IN THE CLOWNS	Sondheim	3

SHOWY DISPLAY SOLOS

61-06	BIRTHDAY BOUQUET	Theme & Variations	4
61-39	• HORSIN' AROUND	Weston	4

6/8 TIME

61-50	• TWILIGHT BELLS	King	4

SPORTS

58-23	• SKATEBOARD (Cross Hands)	Schaum	3

SPRINGTIME

58-52	• APRIL WALK	Levin	3
61-47	• FLOATING IN THE CLOUDS	Nica	4

STACCATO

58-55	• TANGO PIZZICATO	Cahn	3

SYNCOPATION

58-54	• SOMBRERO	Cahn	3
58-58	• WEST INDIES FESTIVAL	King	3

Level Three

All Titles Listed Above are Published or Distributed by Schaum Publications, Inc., Mequon, WI, and are under Copyright